LIVEWIRE
REAL LIVES

return this book on or before the last date
stamped below.

Lauryn Hill

Sarah Blackmore

Published in association with The Basic Skills Agency

Hodder & Stough

A MEMBER OF THE HODDER HEADLI

Acknowledgements

Cover: Katz Pictures

Photos: pp 3, 6 Paul Bergen/Redferns; p 10 Patrick Ford/Redferns; p14 Popperfoto/Reuters; p 16 Kevin Mazur/London Features International; p 20 George DeSota/London Features International; p 24 Hayley Madden/Redferns

Every effort has been made to trace copyright holders of material reproduced in this book. Any rights not acknowledged will be acknowledged in subsequent printings if notice is given to the publisher.

Orders; please contact Bookpoint Ltd, 39 Milton Park, Abingdon, Oxon OX14 4TD. Telephone: (44) 01235 400414, Fax: (44) 01235 400454. Lines are open from 9.00–6.00, Monday to Saturday, with a 24 hour message answering service.
Email address: orders@bookpoint.co.uk

British Library Cataloguing in Publication Data
A catalogue record for this title is available from the British Library

ISBN 0 340 77624 2

First published 2000
Impression number   10 9 8 7 6 5 4 3 2 1
Year   2005 2004 2003 2002 2001 2000

Typeset by GreenGate Publishing Services, Tonbridge, Kent.
Printed in Great Britain for Hodder and Stoughton Educational, a division of Hodder Headline Plc, 338 Euston Road, London NW1 3BH, by Redwood Books, Trowbridge, Wilts

Contents

Lauryn Hill.
Her nickname is L Boogie.
She rose to fame with the group 'The Fugees'.
Now she has a solo career.

She sings.
She raps.
She acts.
She has two children.
She works to help other children.
She has won lots of music awards.
She is a star –
and all before she is twenty-five years old.

1 Early Days

Lauryn was born in 1975.
Her birthday is on 25 May.

Lauryn comes from a big family.
Her grandmother had thirteen children.
Family is very important to Lauryn.

Lauryn grew up with her parents
and her brother
in a town called South Orange.
It is in New Jersey in America.
Lauryn and her parents still live there now.

Lauryn Hill

Lauryn is married to Rohan Marley.
He is the son of a very famous singer
called Bob Marley.
They were married in 1998.

Lauryn and Rohan have two children.
The eldest is a boy called Zion.
They also have a girl.
She is called Selah Louise.

2 A Love of Music

Lauryn has always loved music.
When she was about six years old
she found an old record in her house.
The record was her mother's.
Lauryn listened to it
and thought that it was beautiful.

She says that there was always music
in her house.
Lauryn is just happy to sing –
and always has been.
When she was little she sang in groups
with her friends.
It was a game she loved to play.

Lauryn has always loved singing.

Lauryn has been named by a magazine
as one of the fifty most beautiful people.
She loves clothes and fashion.
She finds it fun to dress up and look sexy.
Can you believe that she was a tomboy
when she was younger?
A tomboy who was really good at back flips.

As a teenager, Lauryn used to hang around
with her brother's friends.
She also spent a lot of time
with her cousins – Wyclef and Pras.

Lauryn formed a group with her cousins.
She was only thirteen.
Pras was fifteen and Wyclef was sixteen.
They called the group 'The Fugees'.

Wyclef and Pras had come to America
from another country.
They were a bit like refugees.
The name Fugees comes from the word 'refugees'.

3 The Road to Fame

Lauryn got her first acting part
when she was fifteen.
She was in a TV show called
As the World Turns.
Soon after she got a part
in the film *Sister Act II*.

Lauryn was also working well at school.
She got a place at university to do a degree.
It was then that 'The Fugees' became famous.

In 1996 they made a record called
'Killing me Softly'.
This song had been a big hit
for a singer called Roberta Flack.
'The Fugees' did their own cover version.
It became the hip hop anthem of 1996.

'The Fugees' at the 1997 Brit Awards.

Lauryn uses her music to talk about her life.
Her songs are about things
that are very important to her.
Lauryn's children are very important to her.

Her son, Zion, was her first baby.
People said that she should not have him.
They said that it was the wrong time
to have a baby.
She should think about her career,
not about having children.

Lauryn wrote a song about her son.
It is called 'To Zion'.
She describes how people
told her not to have him.
They told her to think about it very carefully.
They told her to 'use her head'.

'Lauryn, baby, use your head!
But instead I chose to use my heart.
Now the joy of my world is in Zion.'

4 Lauryn Makes the Big Time

Lauryn's music is so successful.
She has won lots of awards.
In 1999 she won five Grammy Awards.

One of the awards was for
Album of the Year.
It was for Lauryn's album called,
The Miseducation of Lauryn Hill.

'Wow,' said Lauryn when she heard
that she had won.
Lauryn thanked the people
who had worked with her.
She also thanked her family and God.

Lauryn received the Album of the Year Award in 1999.

Lauryn has been named 'Artist of the Year',
'Entertainer of the Year' and
'Best New Artist'.
She also won an award for Best Music Video
for her single 'Doo Wop (That Thing)'.

At one awards ceremony Lauryn chanted
'Respect, respect, respect.'
Her fans and many others
respect her and her music.

You may think that being one of the best
takes up all Lauryn's time.
It doesn't – Lauryn finds time
for lots of other things.

Lauryn with her husband Rohan Marley at the Grammy Awards.

Lauryn spends a lot of time
with her own children.
Families are very important to her.
She also helps other children
and young people.

Lauryn says 'No' to drugs.
She says,
'Drugs, they destroy people.
They destroy lives.
They destroy families.'
She tells young people
to stay away from drugs.

Lauryn also works hard
with her own project.
It is a project to help young people –
to give them chances to do things.
It is called The Refugee Project.

5 The Refugee Project

This project was started by Lauryn.
It organises lots of events
for young people.
Lauryn is very concerned about young people
who do not have the chance
to change the way they live.
She wants to find ways to lead young people
away from drugs and violence.
She wants to find ways
of letting young people do things together
and of mixing with each other.
In this way they will
understand each other better.

Let us have a look at some of the activities
organised through The Refugee Project.

Camp Hill

This is a camp set in the mountains.
It is for young people
aged between ten and thirteen.
They can do lots of activities at the camp.
They can do basketball, storytelling,
music, art, dance, athletics
and lots of other things.
They have their own talent show.
There is also a day for parents
and other family members to visit.
It is called 'Family Day' –
the campers put on a show for the visitors.

Lauryn performing before her fans.

Sometimes Lauryn visits the camp.
One camper said to Lauryn,
'Thank you for taking the time
to come and see me and for sending me.'

Another camper said,
'Thank you for showing me
that young black men can be more in life.'

The Halloween Scare Affair

This takes place once a year.
It is held on 31 October.
It is a time for young people
to enjoy Halloween in a safe way.
The young people dress in Halloween costumes
and have lots of fun.
There is even a haunted house.

The Book Worms Reading Club

This is a reading club for children.
It was set up to help young people read
and to show them that books
can be interesting and fun.

All of the activities in The Refugee Project
are to help young people
who do not have very good lives.
Lauryn says that it is to;
'Change the focus from the richest
to the brokest.'

6 Long-term Goals

Lauryn has done so much.
She has achieved a lot in her music
as well as in other areas.
There are lots of things that Lauryn
still wants to do with her music.

She says,
'Music is so important to me
and how I come across in music
is so important.'
Lauryn is against bad language in songs.
She thinks that music is for everybody
and should be as good as it can be.
Lauryn thinks that there is still
a lot for her to do.
'I wanna always feel
like I can sing this better.'

Lauryn writes, sings and produces her own songs.

Lauryn is very clear about who she is
and what she is doing.
She has shown that she knows
a lot about music.
She did most of the work for her first album
The Miseducation of Lauryn Hill.
She wrote the songs, sang them
and produced the album.

Lauryn has her own film company
and is working on having her own record label.
She wants people to know that as a woman
she can do more than just look good.
She says that it makes her cross
when people ask her more about her lipstick
than her work.

Lauryn's work is not just about her music.
She sees her work as making sure
that people are taken care of.
That people are educated.
That people are healthy and happy.

She believes in God.
She will tell you that her work is for God.

Lauryn has a lot of living to do.
She says,
'I am still living and learning.'
As long as Lauryn is making music,
she will share her learning with us.